The
Trusted Black Girl

*Challenging Perceptions and
Maximising the Potential of Black
Women in the UK Workplace*

By Roianne Nedd

CONTENTS

Acknowledgments

I want to take a moment to acknowledge every single Black Queen who knows the challenges of being a Black woman in the UK workplace but who still shows up and does a fantastic job despite those challenges.

To all the leaders who choose to read books like this to inform and inspire their leadership practice and ultimately make themselves better leaders. I salute you.

To everyone who contributed to this book whether it was by encouraging me to put pen to paper as I wavered and prevaricated, worried that no one would be interested in what I had to say.

The people who believed in me even when I was doubting myself and doubting my vision for this book, the resultant project, and the planned movement.

And last but not least for the women who shared their stories and experiences with me. This movement is for you!

Why is This Book Important?

"As a coach who specialises in confidence, I've lost count of the number of Black women who have shared with me their private stories of feeling lost and overlooked in London workplaces. Even the most progressive employers still haven't got the memo about the need for line managers to be proactive in supporting people of color to counter the million cuts of institutional racism. Sadly, the onus is still on the individual to find the confidence to put herself forward. I hope this book will be widely read by the many great White people who want to help but don't know how."

Kate Franklin
Executive Coach and Director of White & Lime Ltd

"For over a decade I have been running leadership development programmes across the diversity strands, unlocking potential and building confidence. On our courses, we ask participants to share their greatest strengths and achievements which often strikes fear in the hearts of the most humble. When we pull through that barrier and give people *permission* to champion themselves, it breaks open a floodgate of inspiration and greatness. Many are leaders in their communities, award winners, high achieving trailblazers and yet they aren't all progressing at work. What they are doing outside of work is not often reflected by the positions they hold in their careers. The culture of many organisations doesn't consider the skills and strengths people are demonstrating successfully elsewhere. This book is a great tool for managers to evolve into inclusive leaders, who recognise that business success comes from building relationships, inclusivity and actively enabling people to meet their full potential."

Mairi McHaffie
Personal Impact Expert and Director of SceneChange

Introduction

I've known that I wanted to write a book about Black women for a while now, but I wasn't sure about the angle or the tone until I did my podcast with Jonathan Ashong-Lamptey in August 2017. During my interview with him, I talked about my career as a Civil Servant, how I became a Diversity and Inclusion expert and my experiences of being a Black woman in the UK workplace.

As we talked, I recounted numerous examples of me being the person who White people opened up to about race-related issues. Notably, most of these disclosures were unsolicited and sometimes they would be either bordering offensive or utterly offensive. As we talked, I quipped that I must be their "Trusted Black Girl."

After the interview, Jonathan and I had a long talk about the concept of the Trusted Black Girl with him encouraging me to explore the idea in more detail and me deciding at that moment that the book I had always wanted to write would have this title. The book would describe various personas that Black women were perceived as having at work and would also share stories about the experiences of Black women at work in the UK.

I had originally intended to write a dispassionate observational piece, taking an almost clinical and objective view; using the personas to help make the concept relatable. However, life had a different plan for me, and a combination of life experiences and life changes forced me to confront the reality that I had a responsibility to use this book to challenge perceptions of Black women at work and amplify their voices.

Being a Trusted Black Girl had afforded me a level of privilege that I had unthinkingly taken for granted. I was often an insider, someone entrusted with company secrets, someone well respected and dare I say liked and someone who was protected for the most part from personal attacks linked to my blackness.

And it wasn't until I acknowledged this uncomfortable truth that I was able to finalise and publish this book.

As part of my creative process I reflected on all the times that I had been categorised as any other "type" of Black woman and when I deconstructed some of the remarks made to me, and about me it was suddenly clear that there is a fragility about each of the personas that I discuss in this book. Vulnerability because all of them are constructs of other people's views of us, whether society, the workplace, our colleagues or line managers. All these personas are inauthentic because as any Black woman will tell you, at her core, she is nothing but herself, muddling through life like the rest of us and discovering herself every day. There is no persona that we all opt into, but we do all accept whether with ease or unease that we are Black Women.

As part of my exploration of this topic, I posted a blog on LinkedIn offering other Black women the chance to share their stories and experiences. Naively I thought there would be little interest, but in less than 5 days it was shared

"If it doesn't feel right, it may not be, so speak up and challenge the status quo. You just might bring about awareness and positive change."

Lara Yusuf

multiple times and had almost 4000 views with countless women reaching out to me to share their stories and commend me for speaking our truth. If I wasn't sure before their responses would have been enough to convince me, and they further galvanised me into action.

Getting Started

To help you to navigate through this book, I have developed some guidance to get you started. Recognising that there are several reasons to read this book I wanted to explain the four main motivations behind the book.

1. To highlight the typical stereotypes that Black women face in the UK workplace, through the Black Girl Barometer and the persona descriptions which enables Black women to identify which proverbial box or boxes that they may have been placed in and to give leaders the opportunity to think about some common phrases which may have crept into their vernacular.

2. To share case studies based on stories from real women, highlighting how leaders and organisations sometimes get it wrong. **[D&I Practitioners, HR Professionals, Line Managers, and Leaders]**

3. To share essays challenging societal and workplace views of Black women recognising that all experiences will impact on the professional lives of Black women. In fully inclusive workplaces we encourage everyone to bring their authentic self to work but, yet we also often question Black women about choices such as fashion and hairstyle.

4. To provide helpful hints and tips to put things in the workplace right by reducing stereotypes and bias and fostering an inclusive working environment through positive and inclusive leadership practice. **[D&I Practitioners, HR Professionals, Line Managers, and Leaders]**

   Note – some of the tips may seem obvious, tongue in cheek or even patronising but having spoken to countless women over the last year I know that everything I refer to in the book is still occurring in the UK workplace, and so someone out there probably does need even the most basic reminder.

The Black Girl Barometer

As part of the Trusted Black Girl Movement, I encourage Black women to consider whether they have ever been stereotyped into a particular "Black girl persona."

To help you to answer that question I developed the Black Girl Barometer. Tick every statement that someone has said directly to you or you have said to yourself in the workplace to find out if you have a dominant persona.

***Do you lead a team? Consider whether you think you have met any of the women described below. Have you been stereotyping the Black women that you know?

NOTE: *These are not absolutes, and they deliberately lean into stereotypes to illustrate the unfairness of pigeon-holing*

So which Black Girl are you?

Or, which Black Girls do you know?

The Trusted Black Girl – Someone who is often told that people "forget" that they are Black		
1a	Oh yeah, you're Black I forget that sometimes	
1b	You're not like the rest of them	
1c	I am having a problem with <insert the name of a Black person> on my team. It's not because he/she is Black. Can you give me some advice? Do you think I'm racist?	
	I'm not being racist but ……….	

The Not-Black Girl – Someone who is devoid of visible cultural markers that denote any culture apart from "Britishness."		
2a	Why do you refer to yourself as <African/Caribbean/Black etc.> why don't you just say British/English?	
2b	You don't have an accent, or your accent is "posher" than mine	
2c	I don't even think of you as Black, I don't see colour	
The Exotic Black Girl – a woman who appears culturally ambiguous, due to hair or skin tone usually		
3a	You're so light/fair are you sure your mum/dad is Black?	
3b	Oh! I would have never thought of you as Black, are you, Latino?	
3c	You don't look Black you have an exotic look	
3d	Oh! Is that where you're from? I would have never thought you were from Africa	
3e	Your prettiness/attractiveness may be a barrier to your progression	
The Too Black Girl – someone who wears "traditional" or "ethnic" clothing and usually has a natural hairstyle that colleagues will comment on repeatedly		
4a	Why do you wear your hair like that do you think it looks professional?	
4b	That's a very ethnic outfit	

4c	You have quite an urban accent	

The Angry Black Girl – the stereotypical aggressive Black woman

5a	Why are you being aggressive?	
5b	You looked angry in the meeting are you ok?	
5c	I can't believe you're taking offense to this.	
5d	I think you took it the wrong way, maybe you are being over-sensitive	

The Tired Black Girl – a brow-beaten woman who no longer fights against the "system" – the following statements represent likely internal dialogue rather than external comments

6a	I am just here for a few hours a day I will do my time and leave	
6b	No, I don't want to go to the pub with these people they aren't my friends	
6c	I tried to bring that point up years ago it is best I just stay quiet and go home when my day/shift is done	
6d	I can't leave because I don't have the skills necessary to work somewhere else	

The Workaholic Black girl. Always putting in the extra work, doing double what everyone else does for half the reward and very little recognition continually hoping that your hard work will "speak for itself" – this persona is also defined

by a mixture of internal dialogue [ID] and external comments [EC]		
7a	I am sure everyone knows how good I am [ID]	
7b	I don't think you're quite ready for promotion yet [EC]	
7c	I know you can do it (a typical response when the workaholic Black girl attempts to renegotiate workloads and/or deadlines) [EC]	

The Eight Personas

To help illustrate and differentiate between the different experiences that Black women have in the UK workplace, I developed eight personas (N.B. Only seven are represented on the Black Girl Barometer because the final one is a self-identifying persona). These are not exhaustive nor were they scientifically developed. Their purpose is to highlight some of the common stereotypes that exist.

Each persona has been discussed with numerous Black women, and it soon became clear that Black women have been labelled as more than one of these personas at various times in their lives.

The personas also enable us to face the fundamental truth that Black women and indeed most people from a minority group are perceived in ways that are contrary to the way that they represent themselves and highlights the issues of covering, assimilation, and authenticity.

"Covering" in this context refers to the way minority groups often have to pretend to be something that they are not in order to assimilate into the dominant group or culture.

Assimilation refers to the extent to which individuals try to "fit in" to the dominant culture or with the majority group by emulating their behaviours or other factors that influence perceptions of belonging to that group.

Authenticity. In diversity and inclusion circles we speak a lot about "bringing our whole selves to work" but are we really enabling all groups including Black women to be authentic at work? How difficult is it to be yourself when you're a Black woman?

So, let's jump in and examine how Black women are perceived in the workplace and beyond. I wonder if you'll be surprised?

The Trusted Black Girl

Persona Description

The persona that inspired the book. The Trusted Black girl reters to a Black woman who is accepted within her organisation and with limited career progression. Some might call her the "Acceptable Black Girl." She has earned respect from close colleagues but may or may not have a positive reputation across the wider business.

She has gained at least one promotion and is likely to be promoted again. She is valued by her line manager and/or other senior leaders and feels as if success is within her grasp. Her level of comfort with her status as a Trusted Black Girl is situational, and she may or may not have noticed that this is her role in the team or organisation.

> **Insight**
>
> *Success for the Trusted Black Girl relies on her remaining in this persona. She is always just one meeting or conversation away from being reclassified, often to the Angry Black Girl or the Workaholic Black Girl*

Many Trusted Black Girls earn that status because they are educated or naturally intellectual and potentially don't engage with any of the groups or communities that focus on race or cultural issues.

The Trusted Black Girl will be complimented on her accent or lack thereof and her command of the English language. She will likely be able to have conversations about race relations and diversity and inclusion issues without becoming emotional, angry or over-animated.

On a day to day basis, her ethnicity does not seem to impact her career and is rarely a topic of conversation with colleagues. When her ethnicity is highlighted whether, by herself or others, colleagues and leaders are quick to explain to her that they "forget she is Black" or that she "doesn't seem

Black" or "doesn't act Black." This lack of blackness may be commented on by colleagues of all ethnicities including other Black people.

Here is a real conversation that I had with a Black male colleague:

Him: *You're older than me, aren't you?*
Me: *I don't think so*
Him: *You must be*
Me: *Come to think of it no I'm not. Why did you think I was?*
Him: *Because you don't speak "ghetto."*

She may also be asked about her dating preferences with people acting surprised if she has never had an interracial relationship.

She is the person who people confide in when they need to discuss challenges that they may have with other Black people. She is also privy to lots of opinions about Black people some of these may include:

"You're not like the rest of THEM."

"I have always wanted a brown baby" [this is a comment that was made at a work dinner to a Black woman less than 5 years ago]

"Why do all Black single mothers go to church?"

"I don't see colour."

All these comments are problematic, but many Black women who I spoke to said that they were familiar or very similar to comments that they had heard.

Persona Pros

- A heightened level of visibility with colleagues for reasons other than being a Black woman
- More opportunities for development and progression especially those opportunities that involve representing the organisation as you seem to be non-threatening to the status-quo

Persona Cons

- Can create the impression that the lack of "blackness" is being rewarded through career progression and recognition
- The dissonance between how the individual wants to be perceived and how they are perceived
- Isolation from the Black community as they perceive that you have somehow "sold out" to gain traction
- She may be used to represent organisational views that are unpopular with the ethnic minority communities or where a "Black voice" would be reputationally beneficial to the organisation

Inclusive Leadership Tips

If you recognise that there is a Trusted Black Girl on your team consider these things:

- Why you have chosen her to be your sounding board

- Ask yourself whether you have made her working life more difficult by singling her out for special treatment

Top Tip
Avoid attempts to relate to her by referring to Black friends or extended family members. The "I have Black friends" approach does not build rapport and usually has the opposite effect to what you may intend

- Have an open conversation with her about how you relate to her and find out if she is comfortable with the situation.

- Articulate to her and potentially other people, if appropriate, why she is a valued member of your team

- Avoid attempts to relate to her by referring to Black friends or extended family members. The "I have Black friends" approach does not build rapport and usually has the opposite effect to what you may intend

- Consider whether you are holding her back because you have such a comfortable relationship with her and don't want to upset the status quo.

Case study

During a briefing with a senior leader, I supported her when another Black member of staff accused her of making a decision based on race. I knew that it wasn't a racist decision because I had been part of the decision-making process. I also understood why it looked like racism and tried to explain as much to my colleague.

Afterward, the senior leader used me as a sounding board when she needed to make announcements about Diversity and Inclusion or when she was struggling with a Black member of her immediate team. We developed a close working relationship.

"They only picked you because you're Black"

Months later, when a new leadership programme was developed and needed pilot participants she mandated that the programme be tested by a diverse range of future leaders and put me on the programme as the sole Black person.

My direct manager said she wouldn't have chosen me out of all the managers on her team if she had been given a choice and asked me if I wasn't angry because I had only been chosen because I was Black? I wasn't offended, I knew I would smash it and I was glad that I had been handed the opportunity without having to fight or beg for it.

Case Study Commentary

This is a good example of positive action being perceived as positive discrimination. Positive action enables leaders to make decisions which progress a minority group where there is a demonstrable lack of diversity. To create a course that had a fair ethnic mix is not discrimination. Choosing someone with the right level of seniority, from an ethnic minority background and who you believe has the right level of competence and skill is not positive discrimination. It is positive action.

The Not Black Girl

Persona Description

Potentially one of my favourites though slightly controversial The Not Black Girl is likely to have been referred to by the term "Coconut" or "Bounty" whether in front of her face or behind her back. Both descriptions apply to someone who is White on the inside, but brown on the outside think of a dried coconut tor a Bounty chocolate bar.

Within the workplace being perceived as "Not Black" is something that this woman will experience from colleagues of all ethnicities. Black people will find her "too white" or "not Black enough," and other ethnicities will often compare her to other Black people and Black women that they know and draw comparisons about how different they are.

There are similarities to the Trusted Black Girl Persona. People will feel comfortable talking about other Black people with the Not Black Girl. They will ask her for advice on how to deal with other Black people and may even slip up and use derogatory terms to describe Black colleagues because their comfort level with this woman is so high.

The main distinction between the Trusted Back Girl and The Not Black Girl is that the Not Black Girl generally recognises that she is perceived as non-Black but does nothing to dispel the perception. She may also avoid "Black" spaces such as the ethnic minority network or ERG and Black History Month events. This lack of engagement with the Black community may be due to a genuine lack of affinity with these groups and activities, or it may be due to a strategic positioning away from the community.

Persona Pros

- This persona is likely to progress steadily as they will be deemed as non-threatening by colleagues and leaders
- This persona is unlikely to engage in discretionary diversity and inclusion activity so will be more focused on their "day job."
- The Non-Black Girl may progress faster especially in an organisation where diverse hires are being encouraged as she will be deemed to be a safe bet.

Persona Cons

- People are likely to perceive this persona as inauthentic which can have ramifications for corporate trust and career progression
- There may be a level of distrust between this persona and other ethnic minority people which may create tension and friction in the office

> **Top Tip**
> Consider whether you are more comfortable with the Not Black Girl because she emulates white people and therefore seems less threatening or intimidating

Inclusive Leadership Tips

- It is crucial to understand a person's background before assuming that they are being unauthentic
- Do you make similar assumptions of inauthenticity when dealing with a White person whose accent is situational? E.g., I used to work with someone called Sean. He grew up in England and visited family in Ireland for most holidays. Sober Sean speaks with an English accent when he has been drinking and is tipsy or drunk is accent is Irish. Is he inauthentic?
- Ask yourself whether feedback about how articulate she is or her use of the English language is genuine or patronising

26

- Consider whether you are more comfortable with her because she emulates White people and therefore makes you more comfortable

Case study

I was adopted by a White family when I was a baby. My birth parents were both Black. I grew up in a White area, and all my friends from school were white. I only started mixing with Black people when I went to university.

Once I started work, I noticed that lots of people would comment on my

"You're alright. Not like the rest"

accent and say that I was very well spoken and articulate. It was patronising. I also got asked by Black colleagues how I spoke at home and when I told them the same way they looked at me weirdly.

My manager is always saying to me that I am alright and not like the rest and when I ask him what he means he nods knowingly at me. I know he means the other Black people, but I don't understand why he needs to compare us or feels so comfortable talking to me about them. Sometimes he asks me to have a word with them as if all Black people speak some secret language.

Since going to university, I have explored my Black identity more and have a better understanding of what it means to be a Black woman, but I don't know why I have to share these private details about my life to gain acceptance and encourage my boss not to be racist.

Case Study Commentary

- Everyone makes assumptions and has assumptions made about them. Even within the Black community there can be a hierarchy or expectation of blackness
- Inclusion should not rely on people disclosing personal information to gain acceptance and understanding
- Accents can be problematic. Assuming that a Black person who is articulate or has a good command of English is exceptional is inherently biased.
- Pitting Black women against other Black people is racist and reminiscent of the behaviours of the White overseers on slave plantations

The Exotic Black Girl

Persona Description

Oh, this was a fun one to work through. Basically, this description is used for any Black woman who doesn't fit the preconceived beauty standards as held by the person making the statement. What this means is that because I have naturally long hair that which I often wear straight and dark eyes thanks to my Indian grandmother, some people describe me as "exotic looking."

Mixed race women often get told that they look exotic too. It seems to be code for you to look like you are mixed with something other than Black, and the comments come from people of all ethnicities. This particular comment is also often accompanied by comments about physical appearance and attractiveness.

> **Insight**
> Looking exotic may enable you to avoid triggering racial biases if your ethnicity is visually ambiguous

Paradoxically some very dark women with natural haircuts and stylish clothes are sometimes labelled as exotic as well as if their striking attractiveness saves them from being labelled as too Black. Think Grace Jones for instance!

Persona Pros

- Research shows that prettier people get more opportunities
- Looking exotic may enable you to avoid triggering racial biases if your ethnicity is visually ambiguous

Persona Cons

- Some managers will ignore your professional aspirations if you are deemed to be too attractive or exotic looking

- Colleagues may make racially insensitive comments and jokes in your presence as they believe that you are not a Black woman
- You may be hyper-visible because of your unorthodox appearance, and this means that you can ill afford to make a mistake

Inclusive Leadership Tips

- Be conscious about your own biases towards people who appear to be more aesthetically attractive
- Manage your behaviours. Would you comment on the appearance of male team members? Have you ever used the term "exotic" to describe a man?

Case study

One of the managers on my team was leaving, and the job was due to be advertised. I approached my manager to express my interest in the role explaining that my experience in a previous organisation gave me the necessary skills for the role. Her response to me was that it would be difficult for the team to take me seriously if I was promoted above them because I was too attractive.

> **Top Tip**
> **Manage your behaviours. Would you comment on the appearance of male team members? Have you ever used the term "exotic" to describe a man?**

She then further cited that my dress sense was questionable because I had worn a shirt with the slogan "Keep calm and wait for later baby" to an informal team awayday with a casual dress code.

Eventually, they recruited a .an older Black man who was friends with the Director. He smoked cigars, drank way too much at client events, dressed shabbily and had no knowledge of the programme. I wonder if his habits and dress sense were discussed when they considered his interest in the role?

Commentary

Conversations about career progression are often a hotbed for inappropriate an subjective remarks. These may seem innocuous, but they have the impact of influencing the career progression of diverse groups (usually minority groups) and therefore contribute to a lack of diversity at leadership levels and consequently widen the gender and ethnicity pay gaps.

The Too Black Girl

Persona Description

The Too Black Girl wears her blackness like a badge of honour. She utilises various markers of her blackness to emphasise her sense of Black pride, such as a big afro or other natural hairstyles, African print clothing or other cultural garments and she will speak with an accent that suggests she is from somewhere other than the UK and potentially English is only one language that she speaks fluently.

Anyone identifying with this persona may have heard that they have a communication issue so that people don't understand their spoken or written communications. They will also likely have been told that they are sensitive or have a chip on their shoulder. They may have even been accused of racism for sharing candid and negative views about White people or other races.

"I was told that I look very "urban" when I wore a bandana in my hair on dress down Friday"

Another version of the Too Black Girl may be the label that is given to any Black woman who is actively involved in the employee resource group for ethnic minorities. Her knowledge of race issues and eagerness to advocate for change for ethnic minorities may cause some people to describe her as too Black. This label may be given to her by Black people as well as people of other ethnicities.

Persona Pros

- The Too Black Girl reeks of authenticity. She is comfortable in her own skin and makes sure that everyone knows it

- She is likely to understand her own worth and will not be afraid to "sell her skills" in settings such as interviews and pitches
- If nurtured she can become a powerful role model for other Black women and future generations

Persona Cons

- Some people will be defensive towards the Too Black Girl as they expect her to be aggressive and argumentative, so they take pre-emptive strikes at her.
- The Too Black girl may struggle to be heard as people expect whatever she says to be linked to racism or other complaints of discrimination
- Wearing traditional dress is likely to ignite the biases that some people may have and therefore limit career progression.

Inclusive Leadership Tips

- Are you in a position to review the dress code to make sure that it is inclusive of diverse cultures and their clothing?
- Consider why traditional clothes make you feel uncomfortable
- Consider whether comments about appearance are relevant
- Critically evaluate your recruitment processes to see whether people who dress "differently" are being penalised.
- Review publicity material and external facing documents and websites to explore whether they make it clear that diverse cultural clothing is welcomed.

> **Top Tip**
> Consider whether comments about appearance are relevant to the conversation

Case Study

Born in the 1960s, I grew up in a world of change and without apology. Muhammad Ali was telling me "I am the greatest" every time that he spoke. The Cosby show depicted Black excellence and achievement and as time went on, the great writers like Maya Angelou, Dr. Francis Cress Welsing, Bell Hooks. Ntozake Shange, Toni Morrison and Terry Macmillan continued to invoke Black female power. The feminist movement, the civil rights movement, and Black power movements were happening while I was growing in my mother's womb.

As a young adult, my African and health awareness led me to dress, eat and live in a particular way. My visits to Ghana supported my change of style, and corporate suits were made in mudcloth, GTP, and Kente.

In my life as an educationalist, I wore dreadlocks for over ten years and on cutting my locks, I wore wigs, braids and a low natural look. With every look came the comments and the noticeable statements which have stayed with me   These were

"You look very BRIGHT today" when wearing African clothes (UK)or 'I need to put my sunglasses on (Malaysia).'

After wearing wigs for a few weeks in one role, I returned to my braids. I had one manager, the one who had said 'You look very BRIGHT today", say to me that he remembered the first day I came into work in braids! I was taken aback that he had noticed my change of hairstyle

Although this book is the UK focused, it is useful for me to share my experience of working in Malaysia which highlights the global similarities of how I was treated. The globally acceptable standards of beauty begin with White people which means that in many Asian and African countries, there is a culture of skin bleaching. This is a massive problem which causes long-term damage to the epidermis. People actually believe that having white or lighter skin will bring a positive change to their lives.

On reflection, I wonder what the White manager in the UK and the Malaysian manager saw when they looked at me. Was it the friendly happy go, lucky Black woman, sporting her long braids? A woman who they could have a laugh with but who they would not take seriously on the professional platform?

In London, the manager who commented on my clothes, blocked my application when I applied for a promotion within my first year. He reminded me that 'it doesn't work like that here.' For another year, I sat observing the White men who were promoted in their first year. White men for whom 'it did work like that.' I made a decision to move on. I moved to a college where Black people made up the majority of employees, a slight improvement although, the senior managers were all White.

Wearing braids and African clothes will remain a challenge for many who do not perceive this as acceptable 'corporate' or 'professional' wear. A perception that is based on western clothes and hairstyles being 'normal' It is for us to continue to empower and change those perceptions through our impeccable global examples as Black women.

Commentary

Comments about appearance have been frowned upon in relation to skirt lengths and requirements to wear high heels but outrage regarding this type of comment has not stretched to Black women
- Managers who focused on her appearance undermined her sense of value within the workplace and shook her sense of belonging
- People seem to make a correlation between wearing traditional clothes and not being interested in progressing one's career

The Angry Black Girl

Persona Description

This persona will be familiar to so many Black women it is basically the popular stereotype of the Angry Black Woman. The Angry Black Girl is the person who always starts the arguments. We are the person who miraculously is expected to listen to every criticism, every slight and every put-down but do nothing because the moment we react we become the problem and we become the one who is angry.

Notice I am saying "we," I have had my fair share of angry Black Girl moments, but it wasn't until recently that I understood that the Angry Black Girl is a woman at the end of her tether. Most Angry Black Girls have been a different type of Black Girl but sadly the moment

> **Insight**
> The Angry Black Girl is a woman at the end of her tether. Tired of being used and abused and stereotyped.

she steps out or steps up there will usually be someone who questions why she is there, and then the red mist descends, and we are labelled as **that** Angry Black woman.

So, for instance, someone came to meet my boss about a potential collaboration, but she fobbed him off on me. I had to explain all the reasons why we were not going to take a pretty crappy deal from him, and he looked at me getting increasingly agitated and then said "What gives you the right to discuss this with me? I'm not taking that from you". I smiled tightly and explained that firstly I was senior to him so actually I had every right to lead the meeting and considering I was the project manager I had no intention of dealing with such a crap offer. Then my boss comes bustling over telling me to calm down while he skips out of the room. I get angry.

When I went to a pitch meeting and was told by the senior leader that I needed to explain to the project manager lots the changes required to the brief, and he suggested that I should be taking notes so that I recalled his message on verbatim and I smile wryly and explain that I am the project manager. The senior leader doesn't believe it, so he questions how senior I am. It angers me.

Being an Angry Black Girl seems to be par for the course if you're a Black woman. It may not be today, it may not be tomorrow, but one day you will suffer an dignity or an injustice, and it will make you angry, and in a flash, you will have a label that is very difficult to shake. Remember I said that as Black women we are invisible for positive things and hyper-visible for negative things.

It is a bizarre state of mind that you enter when you become the Angry Black Girl because a lot of the time your anger is in response to something real, not an imagined slight or perceived put down. The anger is there because you have been provoked or ironically the anger is there because you have been accused of being angry when you weren't which enrages you, and then you become angry. It's a self-fulfilling prophecy.

Persona Pros

Frankly, I struggled to think of anything positive to say about this apart from:
- If you are the type of person who goes to work to do the bare minimum and doesn't want to do any more than your contracted hours being the Angry Black Girl is likely to buy you a level of UNF*$KWITHABILITY. This means you won't be continually dodging social invites and mindless conversations about your weekend plans and updates about your colleague's children and pets. Being an Angry Black Girl buys you a level of peace.

Persona Cons

- One of the hardest labels to shift in the workplace is that of the angry Black girl. It stays with you and cancels out any good or positive work you have done before even if the good far outweighs the bad.
- Often the angry behaviour is because of an action that someone has taken against the woman, yet that person is rarely reprimanded for their conduct. For some reason, the argument is only deemed to have started when the Angry Black Girl opens her mouth.

Inclusive Leadership Tips

As a leader, it is vital for you to consider the following things before labelling someone as an angry Black Girl

> *Insight*
> *One of the hardest labels to shift in the workplace is that of the Angry Black Girl. It stays with you and cancels out any good or positive work you have done even if the good far outweighs the bad*

- Was she provoked
- How would you deal with someone of a different ethnicity who raised the same issue or behaved in the same way?
- How often does this individual raise queries with you?
- How would you react if someone had treated you the way that she has been treated?

The risk of labelling someone as angry is that you shut their voice down. You make them second-guess themselves and make them fear the way that they will be perceived or the way that you as the person in power will respond. Someone who is always second-guessing themselves and running various scenarios in their head before taking action or making comments is likely to be less productive. All the internal dialogue is taking away from the brain power required to do their job well.

So, what can you do differently?

- Run inclusive meetings where everyone gets the chance to speak
- Take notes when each of your team members is talking so that you can identify who has come up with ideas first and you don't wrongly attribute ideas made by a Black woman to someone else or continuously keep shutting her down while praising others for the same behaviour or approach
- Ensure that one to ones with all staff are of the same quality regarding input from you. Be present with all team members and consider their views.
- Avoid getting involved in hearsay and tattletales. If a team member comes to you with a complaint about another team member rather than have a series of closed-door sessions where you relay the hearsay suggest a joint meeting where you act as mediator and facilitator between the parties.

Case Study

I have a lot of opinions about the work I do because I am passionate about my job. I have frequently come across situations where I am pigeonholed as aggressive or over-sensitive. In a senior team meeting recently we were having a debate about who should take responsibility for an area of work.

A senior director suggested that my team should be leading on this and role modelling what needs to be done in the area of work.

Everyone disagreed openly – when I disagreed I was told "I think you are being defensive about this" to which I replied (and I regret this) "sorry I do not mean to be defensive I just strongly disagree."."

As usual, I had to soften my justified opinion because of the accusation of aggression.

Case Study Commentary

The Angry Black Woman is a common label attributed to Black women in the workplace and beyond. It is triggered every time a Black woman asserts herself, or when she justifiably sticks up for herself. I would say that it is part of the journey of being a Black woman in the UK. Organisations must do more to enable Black women to speak out safely without penalising them and often expecting them to show remorse in order to avoid sanctions.

The Tired Black Girl

Persona Description

This persona is the one that saddens me the most. The Tired Black Girl describes a woman who has been in an organisation for a significant amount of time. She may have had one promotion but is unlikely to have progressed in line with her potential. When she started in her job, she was idealistic and happy and wanted to make a difference.

But then the system broke her. Year after year she watches other people get promoted, people with less experience and people with less to offer often these people look like her manager or have qualities in common with the senior leaders. She soon begins to feel like her "Face doesn't fit."

One day she realises that she isn't happy anymore, she has stopped contributing in meetings, and she no longer offers ideas and solutions to business problems. She clock watches ensuring that the takes every minute of her lunch break and she starts her day exactly at 9am even if it means reading the newspaper at her desk and she leaves at 5pm

> *Insight*
> *She is disillusioned and tired but stays because of financial commitments or because she has resigned herself to her fate.*

on the dot making sure that she doesn't give them even a minute more of her time than she must.

She is disillusioned and tired but maybe stays because of financial commitments or because she has resigned herself to her fate. She is unlikely to engage in any social activity with her team.

Persona Pros

There is very little positive to say about the Tired Black Girl except for the fact that she is likely to suffer from low levels of work-related stress and will not do long hours or extra unpaid work. Her time is her own.

Persona Cons

- She is a wealth of organisational knowledge but is unlikely to share it
- She is an untapped resource with lots of potential that is being unrealised
- Through work-related stress is unlikely being disconnected from work and potentially work colleagues will take an emotional toll
- Disengaging from the organisation fuels stereotypes about lazy and difficult Black people. It is a vicious cycle.

> **Top Tip**
> **Don't assume that a disengaged employee is also a lazy unproductive employee.**

Inclusive Leadership Tips

-When you start leading a new team, observe whether any Black women may fit into this persona.

- Spend time with each team member to consider how they can be re-engaged
- Don't assume that a disengaged employee is a lazy employee
- Consider what the definition of success is for your team and ensure that it includes people who are doing what they are meant to be doing. Discretionary extra effort should not be expected or become the normal standard of performance

Case Study

Have you ever given your all to your work? The late nights, the dedication, sacrificing family time, sacrificing your health! For what?

I spent over 25 years working in the education sector, as a secondary school teacher. I realised each change in my career was because I became tired of the systems around me. The systems that put me into a pigeon-hole, based on others perception of what I was able to achieve.

The final straw came, when I was made redundant from a school, I was making a positive difference in. The school was closed. Despite being overqualified and experienced for the role, i.e., I had

- NPQH (National Professional Qualification for Headship),
- a Masters of Education in School Leadership at a high level,
- experience and knowledge in several roles needed to be a member of the Senior Leadership team] -
- experience being the only deputy headteacher having to complete the roles of several deputies in larger secondary schools,
- good references,
- a mentor to help advice with the application process for Headteachers and Deputy Headteachers roles,

Yet despite all of this each time I applied the door was closed. I would not even get called for an interview! Time and again, my mentor would ask, "When is the interview? What tasks have they asked you to complete?" I would give them the same response. "No reply!"
What did I do in the end?
I stopped applying for the roles I knew, I would make a difference in. Instead, I went and worked in a school as a middle leader.

Even in this role, I had to face challenges of other's perceptions. Everything came to a head in February 2015. One day as I was teaching. I had to face challenges from the students, inappropriate behaviour, lack of support from management and the result? I found myself in the midst of an emotional meltdown. My colleague holding me in her arms as I cried like a baby. Her words, "Not you Ruth. You do not deserve this!"

After months at home recovering, this tired Black women left a profession she loved. Poor health was too great a price to pay.

Case Study Commentary

- Everyone has a breaking point, but Black women are expected to have a much higher threshold for being taken for granted.
- Here was a highly qualified woman who took her experience and knowledge to another organisation albeit in a lower role

The Workaholic Black Girl

Persona Description

Tho Workaholic Black girl is a product of a message that most of us have heard since our childhood. We must work twice as hard as "them" to gain half of the accolades. Anyone woman who has grown up with this messaging is likely to become the Workaholic Black Girl at some point in her career. She works extra hours and takes on extra projects because she truly believes that she will gain success, recognition, and promotion because she has proved herself useful and hardworking.

In the best-case scenario, she will encounter a manager who promotes her by a level or two, never above their level. They will give her some recognition for her efforts but never as much as she deserves. But sadly, not even this mediocre reward for a job well done will be offered to many Workaholic Black Girls. Many of these women are trapped working for managers who happily use their talent and skills and their willingness to do extra. They give them extra work with the most promise of progression and promotions that don't come. This unethical manager may even provide bonuses for a job well done, but these payments are designed to keep the workaholic Black girl exactly where she is.

Workaholic Black Girls appear in every workplace and are prone to become Angry Black Girls if they realise that they are being exploited and duped or if they realize that they will never progress despite all their hard work and commitment.

Persona Pros

- The Workaholic Black Girl has a range of skills which are transferrable if she decides to leave the organisation
- The Workaholic Black Girl can build a reputation within her organisation as a go-to person and use this to get out from under an unhelpful manager
- She also uses her knowledge to give her a sense of confidence underpinned by her competence.

Persona Cons

- The Workaholic Black Girl is prone to stress and burnout. Often burning the candle at both ends and potential juggling family life she may be at a higher risk for eventual sick absence
- She can also suffer from low levels of engagement with her workplace if she figures out that she is being used
- Workaholic Black Girls often find out hard to say no once they are trapped in the cycle of saying yes. They think that if they say no then that will be the thing that stops them from being promoted.

> **Top Tip**
> Explicitly articulate what high performance means to you as a leader and ensure that your whole team knows how they can demonstrate reward-worthy performance

Inclusive Leadership Tips

- Ensure that you have an objective way to assess and balance team workloads? This may be through work allocation forms or work returns
- Think about whether one particular person gets all the menial work? Using work allocation records, reflect on whether some people get all the low-value tasks. Are those people the Black women?
- Explicitly articulate what high performance means to you as a leader and ensure that your whole team

knows how they can demonstrate reward-worthy performance.

Case study

Until recently I was the only Black female in my organisation. I work really hard at what I do because I enjoy what it and I have always really wanted a career where I can progress and do well. I am frequently told that I am great and I get excellent appraisals. I have taken on projects that others would not do or could not do to try to demonstrate my ability. I work long hours and weekends and always try to meet a deadline.

I feel there is an expectation that I can just get the work done despite heavy workloads. I have observed that others in my team get additional support particularly if there is a risk of someone leaving due to having too much on or being over-stretched. I find this problematic and frankly galling as I would never threaten to resign because of a heavy workload because it goes against my strong work ethic I have asked for additional support, but this always seems to be ignored or de-prioritised.

"How come it took so long for them to promote you?"

My peers have consistently been promoted before me despite me being in the organisation for a longer period of time and consistently exceeding in my appraisals. I have had peers comment 'how come it took so long for them to make you a manager/promote you?

I recently became frustrated with this and tried to have a discussion with my line manager (A white, male). I was told that I shouldn't compare myself to others and that his expectations are just a lot higher than other managers regarding the criteria for promotion and he just didn't think I was ready. I tried to get him to explain to me what I needed to do to demonstrate that I had the right skills to be working at a higher level.

The explanation was unclear and lacked direction. I asked other senior directors the same question and was met with blank faces and reassured that I was a great employee.

I have just recently been promoted in my current organisation, but it has felt like a struggle to get there, and when it did happen, it felt long overdue.

Case Study Commentary
- Black women must meet an often higher and invisible standard of performance.
- They are often treated like work horses, doing copious amounts of work without breaks and with the expectation that they won't complain
- The Angry Black woman is a trope that is levelled at nearly every Black woman at some point in her career and especially when she stands up for herself. It is usually used punitively

The ? Black Girl

Persona Description

The ? Black Girl describes Lesbian and Bisexual Black women and reflects the various labels and assumptions that are made about them at work. These women belong to the LGBT+ community, the Black community, and the sisterhood. But what are their experiences? To find out and develop this persona I created a survey and spoke to some of them.

The first thing I found out was that perceptions of the ? Black Girl was often linked to her appearance. There seem to be three groups that emerged yet to illustrate the complexity only two of these groups are LGBT+ Black women.

1. Feminine women who everyone assumes must be heterosexual because of their femininity
2. More masculine women who are treated with a sense of morbid curiosity or like one of the lads or approached with a level of confusion
3. Black women with Bald or low-cut hair who may or may not LGBT+ but who get treated as if they were.

It was also interesting that the challenges came from other Black people as well as other races and the inappropriate comments/behaviours when identified were pan-racial.

Personas Pros

- The women who are out at work have largely positive experiences which may be because the type of workplace that enables them to be out is also one where negative behaviours will be nipped in the bud.
- Anyone who can be authentic and be themselves will feel a stronger sense of self and self-confidence than someone who has to pretend to be something that they are not.

- Being out at work may act as a counterbalance for some of the cons of being perceived as an Exotic Black Girl

Persona Cons

Through the survey, respondents gave some examples of how they are treated at work. These included:

- "Femme invisibility exists. Because I do not fit the stereotypical look of a lesbian, some people just assume I'm straight and then make conversation with me about how disgusted they are with people who are a part of the LGBT community. It can be very uncomfortable at times. As well as this cultural barriers also play a role in the workplace as being Black and gay is still not highly accepted."

"Hire more Black people. My lesbianism ranks second in importance but having other Black colleagues will at least relieve some of the tension. I can't relate to White lesbians so hiring more lesbians would be pointless""

- "Most of the comments have referred to my race, e.g., a manager wanting to call me V-Dawg."
- "Being masc people make assumptions about my character. E.g., Aggressive/angry. Usually means I am left alone, but I'm happy with that.
- "People treat you like an alien because they act as if they didn't know that Black lesbians exist."

Inclusive Leadership Tips

- Avoid showing awkwardness around the topic. Check your behaviour and compare it to how you treat other colleagues why do Black gay women get treated differently is it their blackness, their gayness or their gender that is the issue?

- Stamp out homophobic language and behaviour in the workplace
- Create more open environments for challenge, discussion and education don't go straight to sanctions
- Think about the scope of the D&I policy. Have you considered that Black Lesbian and Bisexual women are a distinct group with different needs to Black women and different needs to lesbians and bisexual women?
- Think about the small talk that happens in the office. Questions about weekend plans and partners can often "out" people or make them feel uncomfortable if they aren't out at work. As a leader, you shouldn't be part of the problem. Adopt more inclusive language and ask more inclusive questions or share your story and then wait for others to share what is comfortable for them.

Commentary
Organisations are still struggling to understand how feminism can be intersectional and struggle to look at their gender approach with a multi-cultural lens, so it seems like understanding how to include Black Gay and Bisexual women is just a bit too much like hard work. Advice for organisations is to enable people to define what they need, ensure that structures for women embrace all women, structures for LGBT+ people cater for all ethnicities and that ethnic minority communities are set up to welcome LGBT+ people in the workplace.
Collaboration between networks and employee resource groups must not only be encouraged but should be mandated through shared resources and clear accountabilities for inclusion within their

The Successful Woman

Persona Description

The successful Black Woman persona is the holy grail. It is what we all want to achieve. It is important to note that this persona does not even include the word Black. Even though we are Black women, we want to be recognised for our success without being defined by our colour, our sexual orientation our family situation or our beauty. We want to be recognised for our awesomeness.

Critically there are three things which these successful women have in common
1. They are authentic at work and home
2. They have achieved a level of work/life integration that works for them
3. They have respect from peers and senior leaders and wield positional power and wide-reaching influence within the organisation.

The three crucial elements of success are intrinsically linked. Women who have built strong reputations and who have the ear of the highest people in the office are able to manage their work life in such as way that it integrates with their home life more harmoniously. I deliberately refer to work/life integration as these days it is unlikely that you are ever completely switched off from either one. And frankly, balance suggests half and half which is unlikely.

Authenticity is also an important aspect for the successful woman. Authenticity enables her to embrace and share her true self, and in so doing her concept of success is defined by her rather than by someone else.

You will recognise the successful Black women in your workplace because they will receive accolades and recognition as role models and leaders for staff of all ethnicities and genders.

Persona Pros

- A successful woman will exude confidence and comfort in her own skin. She won't feel the need to justify herself or her existence, and she will be very self-assured.
- A successful woman has strong personal boundaries and is in touch with her values by integrating them into her work to create a sense of belonging for her and others who share those values.

Persona Cons

- A woman who has achieved success at work is likely to strive for the same level of success elsewhere once she feels she has achieved corporate success. This may lead her to look for something more fulfilling such as voluntary work or work with a social purpose but may also lead to a sense of dissatisfaction at work that cannot be assuaged.

> **Top Tip**
> Accept that Black women sometimes have different personas at work and home. Both personas, no matter how different they may be are an authentic fake if you witness her switching behaviours depending on the group that she is interacting with.

Inclusive Leadership Tips

As a leader, it is your responsibility to help unleash the full potential of the people who report to you. Some ways to help Black women to achieve success is through these steps:

- Ask them what success means to them
- Consider whether you have any preconceived views about how far they can progress and then remove these views from your mind.
- Create the space for them to share their personal situation with you so that you can understand what work/life integration looks like for them. Note: if they

56

do not want to share personal information that is equally acceptable for them not to.

- Accept that Black women sometimes have different personas at work and home. Both personas no matter how different they may be are an authentic version of her so don't judge her as being insincere or fake if you witness her switching behaviour depending on the group that she is interacting with.

The Successful Woman Case Study – Michelle Delices

Introducing Michelle Delices. Michelle is a senior leader in one of the world's largest hospitality firms. She reports directly to the regional director and is a respected senior leader within the organisation.

When I started to write this persona, I knew that it wouldn't necessarily be easy to find a real-life Black woman who has achieved success without seemingly sacrificing a facet of her life. Many women, myself included feel like Black women just can't have it all, we can't have the relationship, the children and the career. Something has to give. So, when I met Michelle and got to know her, I was in awe, and I knew she would be the profile.

Michelle is a woman who works in an operational part of the business. Considering the personas, I have witnessed Michelle wear headwraps sometimes, change her hairstyle frequently and command an agenda on diversity with the same ease as the way she delivers presentations about her day job.

As a senior leader, Michelle is expected to "talk the talk" on diversity and inclusion, but she also "walks the walk," committing resources to diversity and inclusion initiatives and challenging the leaders to do the same. As a Black woman, it would be easy for Michelle to only focus on race and gender, but she has initiated work to help colleagues recognise and mitigate unconscious bias all while delivering commitments to her day job.

Michelle has even received accolades for her role model status including most recently in the Financial Times. She is proud to be a role model for Black people and even more specifically for Black women.

But it isn't just Michelle's professional life that makes her a success. Michelle also single-handedly brought up her son. While he was growing up, she was a hands-on mother balancing work commitments with her maternal duties. Then she achieved the final part of the trifecta and got married holding down a happy relationship as well as being a mother and a successful career woman.

Most importantly when I consider Michelle's story, I think it's essential that you all know Michelle was not born with a gold spoon in her mouth nor did she get handed things on a silver platter. Like her son, she was brought up by a single mother and achieved her success because she worked hard, didn't give up and was clear about her aims and objectives both personal and professional.

Michelle isn't just successful because she has a career, a child and a husband Michelle is successful because she defined what her success looked like and she went for it.

Success is in the hands of the beholder!

Case Study Commentary
Black women progress when they have sponsorship from a senior leader especially a White male senior leader
- Working environments that enable people to be authentic help them to make huge professional impact
- With the right organisational culture Black women can achieve a level of balance between personal and professional commitments and excel at both

Contributor Persona - The Everyday Black Woman

The response to this book has been overwhelming and sparked lots of comments and discussions. One comment stood out to me because it presented an additional persona. Here's what one Black woman had to say after talking to her friends about the personas that I developed.

****

"I would label myself "The everyday Black woman,"
- Culturally aware
- Wears weave because it's easy to maintain and switch.
- Not aggressive but will appropriately question an ignorant comment towards her culture or ethnicity within the workplace,
- Ambitious,
- Confident,
- Able to communicate flexibly dependant on the audience
- Works hard will go that extra mile in situations where recognition of contribution and skill are acknowledged
- Generally, operates well
- Seems to be respected by her peers within the workplace

****

The Black Girl Essays and Commentary

When writing this book, I thought that it was essential to hear the voices of different women and to consider the experiences of Black women from different perspectives and in a context that was ins some cases wider than the workplace.

These essays bring together different voices including my own on thought-provoking experiences and questions.

People will often put you in a box!

Remember: No matter how nice the box is...

1. You weren't born in a box
2. Use the tools and resources you have already to build yourself up, in preparation to move on always have to hand:
   - **A Drill** - to drill holes in the box so you have air to breathe
   - **A Saw** - to cut out a doorway to leave but, allows you shelter if storms are raging around you

Most Importantly, it is essential you have
   - **A Hammer** – to construct something of your choice, not what someone else creates for you!

Being a Black Woman in a White Corporate World

Roianne Nedd

Binge watching the Apprentice 2017 and watching how Joanna was perceived and treated only strengthened my resolve to publish this book. I wanted it to explore the perceptions and experiences of being a Black woman in the UK workplace and gives practical tips to managers and organisations about recognising and checking bias.

Watching Joanna be labelled as too outspoken and argumentative was oh so familiar. The "Angry Black woman" label is much more widely used than people admit and covers any emotion that moves beyond docile or acquiescent.

Then the most frustrating thing is that any attempt to stick up for yourself is deemed as "making excuses," "paranoia" or even "going on about things." Joanna's experiences proved this week after week until finally, she stopped trying to make her voice heard and accepted the constant sniping and put-downs of her fellow contestants even crying from the sheer frustration and unfairness of it all.

And that was the turning point and sadly highlights another classic example of how Black Women are treated. Once Joanna cried and showed "remorse" for being argumentative she suddenly became more acceptable and "human" in the eyes of the judges and interviewers. What's sad is that this behaviour is clearly tied to colonialism where Black Women were treated better in direct proportion to them behaving well and not challenging their situation.

It's sad that despite people claiming that slavery is in the past there are still numerous examples of how the thought processes and privileges gained during slavery and colonialism still colour the experiences and perceptions of many people. Both Black and White people and people from other ethnicities have, over the years, chosen sides and experienced differing versions of discrimination and progression (but that's a different topic)

In 2018 I hope that conversations about equality take a more intersectional approach so that we stop using the BAME label to hide the lack of progression and so that we consider how gender intersected with race has differing impacts for ethnic minority men and women. It's time for a change, and it's time for more empathy and awareness!

****First published on LinkedIn in December 2017

Beware of the Hair – The Hair Hazard

Roianne Nedd

In the infamous words of India Arie "I am not my hair." Black women's hair is constantly under scrutiny both within and outside the workplace. Natural hair versus processed hair, to weave or not to weave, headwrap or head tie? The choices and possibilities are endless. When we add the complexity of workplace dress codes, expectations and management preferences to the conversation things can get complicated, confusing and annoying.

In recent times some organisations, recruiters and managers have included hair requirements when speaking to Black Women. Questioning the professionalism of Afros, braids, and headwraps. The challenge here is that the standard of acceptable hairstyles has been set against a European ideal. Even natural hair is often seen as more acceptable when styled in a European fashion such as French twists or chignons.

These formal hair challenges follow decades of debate and conversation about Black hair both male and female and what defines acceptable in the workplace.

To prove my point here is a list of comments that Black women have had directed to them about their hair in the workplace. (all collected on Facebook)

Is it real?

Is it all yours?

Can I touch it?

Do you wash it?

What do you do to get it to look like that?

I wish my hair could look like that it's so cool?

'Your hair is amazing."

'How do you get your curls so small?"

I want my coils to be tight like yours, so I can rock an afro too

You've got that 'good' hair. you must have Indian / white in your family

You can do so much more with your hair

How long does your hair take to dry?

what do you put in it?

I love your afro

It's so soft. Can I touch it?

Does it hurt when you put it like that (cornrows)?

It looks tight.

How long does it take to comb?

I wish my hair could do that

You've really changed.

What made you change your hair?

It's really different

Your hair doesn't grow, does it?

Consider This

The list above is fairly long. Would the list be the same length if we were thinking about comments that White women hear about their hair?

Why do Black women face this level of scrutiny about a fairly simple every day part of their appearance?

Imagine how distracting it is for Black women to deal with these comments instead of getting on with their jobs.

Black Women as Role Models – Leading the Ethnic Minority Women

Tanya G

Within the UK STEM market, a lot of emphasis has been placed on encouraging students from diverse ethnic backgrounds to take up the STEM subjects. While many students from an Asian background study STEM subjects, the uptake is lower from other ethnic backgrounds. It is often even rarer for women from a minority background to study a STEM subject and to then progress into a linked career. This makes me something of a unicorn in this field as I am an Asian woman who studied STEM and has built a career using my STEM skills and qualifications. This has therefore made finding Asian female role models within my field fairly difficult, and it is why I have observed that my professional role models are Black women who blazed the trail but are still under-represented within the rail industry.

To date, I have worked with two Black female role models within my career. One of whom I went to university with and the second who I met at an engineering consultancy firm. As a woman in engineering, I feel there is no shortage of female role models in the STEM sector. However, as an Asian woman of Indian origin, it is rare for me to meet and work with other ethnic minority females in my industry. Therefore, to meet other women who have the same interests as me and who have a similar background is both unusual and of value.
There are many Indian males in my sector, as well as Asian (Chinese, Japanese, etc.) role models but no Indian women that I know of.

The lack of cultural role models is why my two Black female colleagues are role models to me and not just because they are ethnic minority women. There are two predominant reasons why I admire them, and I am grateful to have had the opportunity to work with them.

..rstly, it is their technical abilities and interests, and resultant career progression. It demonstrated to me and everyone else that women and especially minority women have the same technical expertise as everyone else. They have proved that the lack of representation isn't about talent.

Secondly, they both have an abundance of confidence. They have held true to their ambitions and their career paths and have managed to strike a balance between understanding the significance of their gender and ethnicity while also being unfettered by their double minority status and making the issue of diversity irrelevant to their career trajectories.

The lessons I have learned from them
1. The value of following my technical interests first and foremost. This, in turn, leads to career progression based on ability and merit, rather than having to play the race or gender card to get career progression by helping a company can show they are fulfilling a quota.

2. The other key lesson I have learned from them is that background and heritage are important. Their backgrounds influence their perspectives, and if an organization truly values diversity, they will appreciate the filter that comes with having a different background. This means that my background is relevant because it influences my thought process and the way I approach problem-solving. It is because of these differences and how they affect my thinking that I am able to provide unique solutions which may have the potential to address a long-standing or complex issue more favourably than someone else. That isn't to say that I will always produce a solution that is significantly different to that of a White female or Indian male, but I am likely to have approached the issue from a different angle which enables a wider

context to be gained which highlights something that may have otherwise been missed.

In closing, I just want to take a moment to appreciate the impact that these two role models have had on my career and to extend a hand to any Asian females in STEM who may, like me be suffering from a lack of visible role models. Why not connect with me on LinkedIn so that we can show the next generation that we do exist.

My Language: A Barrier to my Success

MaryFay Tita-Kuna

You feel trapped, frozen in your own skin as you are asked a question. Instinctively your response is a stutter from a blank mind. There is a struggle to resonate with your colleagues, because of the anxiety that overwhelms you, in fear you will communicate the wrong thing. Next comes a powerful blow to your confidence after you're asked to repeat yourself, because 'they can't understand' what you're saying. Then comes repetition of the voices in your head; asking your thoughts 'if they make sense?'

Every time you step foot through those doors at work, the paranoia nudges you, reminding you of the disparity in your ability to communicate as effectively as your colleagues. I understand. I understand the power of identity through language and how for many of us Black women, it has been a barrier to success in the workplace and outside of it too.

For many years, Black women have been in a continuous battle to be understood. Many have fallen victim to their intelligence being underestimated, leaving them feeling ostracized in their work environments. Floella Benjamin in her book 'Coming to England' explicitly highlights her experiences; where she states "our individual identity was never acknowledged. We had come from different islands- Jamaica, Barbados, Grenada, St Kitts, Dominica, and Antigua- and spoke with different accents."

In this book, she describes her difficult integration experiences after migrating to England, during the Windrush period from Trinidad. The numerous references her book makes to language and accents drew my attention to the importance of it in relation to cultural adaptation. Benjamin gives an account of a time she was stopped mid-sentence when reading to her class at school and called a "guttersnipe" by her teacher. She was told if she wanted to remain in the class "she will learn to speak the Queen's English." Imagine the psychological effect that being skinned of your identity in public can have on such a young child. Unfortunately for some of us, it will be an experience more veristic than imaginative.

"Let me give you a tip. You wanna make some money here? Use your white voice"- Sorry to Bother you (2018)

The concept of westernizing your identity in exchange for better opportunities is a proverb overly recited, not only amongst the surroundings of the average Black women, but also in her mind. Linguistic profiling was researched by John Baugh in 2016, a Professor of Education & Linguistics at the University of Stanford, highlighting the discrimination faced by people of color when calling companies for employment or housing opportunities. Baugh states, "generally speaking the minority dialects do not fare as well, particularly in the affluent communities." The voices that sounded more ethnic, were less likely to have successful outcomes. The conclusion from Baugh's research is a reflection of the daily struggles faced by people of color, conveying the message that the identity of a Black person is less valuable. The voice of a Black person is less important.

Furthermore, a research publication on priming identity and biracial speech by Gaither et al. concluded, "Individuals with multiracial identities face unique challenges in navigating the social landscape, by adopting specific cognitive strategies that enable them to associate more with one racial identity as needed." (Gaither et al., 2015). The negative profiling of Black speech and identity suggested by these publications provide an explanation as to why, "just 3.5% non-white faces at the top of the UK's leading 1,000+ organisations, compared with 12.9% in the general population.

The scarcity is much worse along gender lines, with less than a quarter of those BAME positions of power occupied by women." (The Guardian & Operation Black Vote, 2017). If Black women are prone to discrimination just because of the way they sound, as opposed to their character, it consolidates the argument that language is a barrier to success.

The Journey to Inclusivity in Melanin

"Whenever a conscious Black woman raises her voice on issues central to her existence, somebody is going to call her strident, because they don't want to hear about it, nor us. I refuse to be silenced, and I refuse to be trivialised, even if I do not say what I have to say perfectly." – Audre Lorde

If Black women are to break linguistic barriers, they must first of all be heard. They must be valued and not ostracized. The voices of Black Women have been a source of empowerment to many around the world, from Oprah Winfrey to Michelle Obama. It is important to not be afraid, to move to the front of that boardroom meeting, to volunteer to lead that presentation, because you have something to offer. Your voice is the organ to your soul, orchestrate your melody.

Pariah

Catherine I

In my 18+ years of working life, I have transitioned from a junior position to a Head of/Director position. In the early days, life was easier as it was accepted that me, as a Black woman would be a junior member of the team in most workplaces.

However, I noticed, as I climbed the corporate ladder, that being accepted as an educated Black female, in whatever workplace I happened to be working in at any time was becoming much harder especially as I was promoted into more senior roles.

Having a team introduced me to a whole new level of poor treatment which began with snide comments being made between members of my team during team meetings. Knowing glances, loaded with sly and vindictive intentions, passed from one team member to the other and sniggering during team meetings at the point where I was addressing the team became the norm.

Initially, I viewed these transgressions as isolated incidents of poor behaviour, unprofessionalism and a desire to be unruly. However, as I continued to climb the corporate ladder, I realised that there may well be a more disturbing reason for their behaviour. My teams have always been European. I have managed international teams both in the UK and in Europe and have been responsible for a mix of both males and females; sometimes younger and sometimes older than me.

Some were indifferent but most – specifically the teams in Europe – were not keen to be managed by a female and particularly not keen to be managed by a Black female, who was educated and had a good sense of her own mind and the direction in which the business wanted her to take the team.

This discomfort manifested itself in a few ways – some of which I've already mentioned above associated with what could be summarised as bad manners – laughing when I was talking, giving each other knowing glances while I was talking or even ignoring me as I was talking and using laptops or phones during team meetings.

The other manifestations were a little starker and came in the shape of not greeting me in the morning despite me greeting them first, going out to lunch and not inviting me or having secret meetings where they would discuss my performance and, what could only be described as, plot against me. I have been systematically targeted many times in my career for basically doing what I have been hired to do – complete the tasks and manage the team.

Quite often the team resented being told what to do but, when confronted by a White, male manager or even a White female manager they would gladly do as they were asked. On one occasion, I asked my team to ensure they did not work from home on the same days of the week as on certain days there would be no member of the team in the office. I was polite and respectful in making the request and made it clear that this would not stop them from working from home two days per week if they so wished.

This request was met with outrage and disgust the likes of which I have never witnessed before in my time as a manager. The team quickly organised a revolt and gathered to individually complain about me to my line manager.

This has happened to me more times than I care to recall. Members of my team going to the manager above me to complain about me for basic matters which would normally be dealt with easily within the confines of the team. What always surprised me the most was the willingness of the senior manager to take on board what the team was saying without checking with me first. The willingness of the, always European, senior manager to believe and sympathise with subordinate team members always astounded me.

In many of my workplaces (particularly those where I have held a senior position and some level of power), I have been routinely ignored, "sent to Coventry" or excluded from social events, even work meetings. Many times, I discovered that my email address was 'accidentally' missed when invites went out.

MDs and CEOs have routinely ignored my requests to meet (even when the meeting has been mandated by the company as part of my induction). I even messaged one senior marketing leader when he was showing as online and available at the time we were due to meet to find out where he was, but I was just ignored and disregarded. I had to chase his PA only to discover that the meeting had been cancelled but no one, it seemed, deemed it necessary to inform me.

You might pity them or even me, but this type of experience is routine, regular and pervasive, endemic and perhaps even inescapable as a Black woman at work

She is Violent in Meetings, and I Feel Unsafe Around Her
Mbeke Waseme

I looked at the hijab-wearing woman with the UK accent. We had met at a conference and had laughed and joked at the joys of meeting another person who had worked overseas. The daily navigation of body and verbal expression was hard when one worked as an expatriate. People spoke English in their own way, but there was nothing like meeting someone who was from the UK and who had the same experiences.

I had found myself falling in love with a man in Ghana for this same reason. After years of watching my words and being mindful of what I said while living there, I had found a friend who was from the UK and of Jamaican parentage too. Our conversations could go on for hours, and even though exhausted, I always felt high on the sharing.

On this occasion, she sat in the meeting looking smaller than her already tender frame. ***"She is violent in meetings, and I feel unsafe around her"***. I could hear these words going around in my head. The representative from Human Resources didn't say much. He was almost 70 and looked as if life had dealt him a raw deal. This was his opportunity for steady employment, and he didn't plan to mess it up. He would shuffle around the building helping people with their problems or creating some. *" What exactly happened?"* he asked my accuser *"She was violent towards me in January and in September,"* she confirmed hanging her head from the pain.

"What did *you* do?" He asked with the enthusiasm of someone who wished they were elsewhere but also with the good sense to assume that there had been some provocation. A silent response led Mr. HR to turn to me "What happened in January and September?", He enquired. I smirked as I was finding the whole situation comical. *"I cannot remember in detail what happened last week. January was a year ago"*, I responded, aware that my bemusement could be interpreted as nonchalant. "I understand," he said keeping his composure. Although he too wanted to smile. *"What about September?" he asked me.*

In September I had reflected on my unacceptable response to Mandilah and had left her a note and tried to speak to her. Neither of these had received any follow-up, so I concluded that she was not interested in resolving this. I was surprised to be called to this meeting, I stated in my most surprised and concerned voice.

"OK. Thank you", He responded now only going through the motions. *"Why were you like that?",* Mandilah turned to me and asked. *"I am sorry that you experienced it so harshly. That was not my intention".* She stretched out her hand. The shake was formal. It reminded me of the shake from a man who has just won the war. I was shocked at the feel of the cold hard hand. *"Is there anything else Mandilah?* Mr. HR asked. *"No. I am happy that she has apologised and I have accepted it!"*

This was a newly energised woman. Energised on the act of bringing (or definitely trying) to bring another person down.
I walked out of the meeting feeling shaken. African women like me who open our mouths and speak without apology are told by the world we are violent and aggressive. As human beings, we are generally afraid of those who we perceive to be violent and aggressive. Those words had shut many of us down. For of course, why would we wish to be seen in this light?

The last year had been the usual range of activities for our team, and the meetings had seen Ms. Hijab as vocal and troublesome as usual. Some had stopped challenging her for fear of being dragged into her tennis match where only her rules worked. It is funny for we had been friends for a brief moment, visiting museums, laughing and chatting. How quickly that had changed.

Swipe Left to Feed Your Bias, Swipe Right to Feed Your Fetish

Roianne Nedd

Online dating has reached the pinnacle of convenience. These days apps allow you to indicate your interest or lack thereof with a simple swipe of the screen. Swipe left if you're not interested and swipe right if you are.

To make these choices we are using the most rudimentary tool, instant physical attraction. Research and commentary have shown that these apps have become a breeding ground for racism wrapped in a cute little package of preference. Every day people are swiping left just because the colour of someone skin doesn't please them or maybe they are swiping right because they have a fetishized view of skin colour.

Yes, in this day and age men still fantasise about Black women. I have had friends tell me that men have told them just looking at the deep brown colour of their skin is appealing, and I can't count the number of times that men on dating apps have described me as Black and beautiful always adding my skin tone to any compliment that they give me.

But I digress. The issue that I really want to talk about is that the world of swiping for preference goes a long way to reinforcing biases. With no attempt to introduce non-physical attributes we are relying on our stereotypical views, and past experiences of people who look like the dating pool to make decisions and bias like any muscles gets stronger the more we use it. So, the more we use our biases to discern the groups who we find attractive the more our bias grows.

Now I know I know this book looks mainly at the workplace, but I believe there are implications for the workplace. Imagine I am swiping left on the way to work each morning, busily strengthening my biases, and then I come to work, and

I have to make decisions that relate to people. Maybe I'm sitting on a recruitment panel interviewing Black women and white women. Is my brain unconsciously swiping left as I interview the Black woman because that isn't my preference?

I haven't done any research in this area, I am just sharing my humble opinion that online dating may be increasing the likelihood of biased decision-making in relation to Black women at work.

Visibility, Diversity, and Tokenism: Confessions of a Black Sign Language Interpreter

Tricia Mitchell

I've been fortunate. I spent eighteen years working in a field that was historically oppressed and experienced discrimination. While the oppression of minority groups within marginalised communities does occur, I, personally, wasn't aware of any stereotypical perceptions of me as a Black woman working with, and within, the Deaf community.

That is until I freelanced as a sign language interpreter.

This essay explores the dichotomies of being both highly visible, because there were so few Black sign language interpreters north of Birmingham, and invisible, due to people's mental constructs of what an interpreter looked like. Being approached solely on the basis of being a Black interpreter, by organisations who desired to reflect equality and diversity, while the very nature of the requests was inherently tokenistic.

Being Visible

I recall one of my first call outs to interpret for the Police. For years, I refused requests to interpret because I wasn't qualified. Once qualified, I lacked experience in legal interpreting. I kept declining the call out requests out of integrity and fear until I learned that other interpreters with less experience or skill were accepting police assignments. I knew I could do a better job. It was time to bite the bullet.

My phone rang after midnight, waking me up. A Deaf man was in police custody. He'd been arrested on suspicion of drink driving and had refused a roadside breath. They couldn't put him on the Intoximeter machine until they'd read him his rights and needed an interpreter to convey everything in sign language.

When I arrived at the police station, I found it difficult to understand him. My tired mind wondered if he had minimal language skills, but then he'd sign 'What's my constitution?" My addled brain was trying to reason that someone with basic language skills wouldn't know the word 'constitution.' As we stood by the Intoximeter machine, he stalled sufficiently by deliberately miscommunicating that once we were satisfied, he understood his rights, he blew under the limits.

For days afterward, I questioned my ability, especially as I knew my cognitive functioning was optimal during daylight hours. Meanwhile, a friend of mine "reported back" on how a man at the Deaf club was bragging about how he had pulled the wool over the Black interpreter's eyes! He was sharing with his mates how to fool interpreters to get off a potential drink-driving charge.

The confidentiality clause in my profession's Code of Ethics didn't allow me to confirm or deny being there, but we both knew that I was the only qualified Black sign language interpreter in the area. Initially, I was livid at the man, as I'd wasted so much time berating myself. Then I softened as I realised he was doing what most people would do when backed into a corner. It wasn't personal; he was using whatever trick in the book he could.

Using a visual language that causes people to remark, "Oh, I learned sign language at school, but I can only remember the alphabet" - and being Black meant that I was highly visible. [Deaf] friends would discreetly share with me when and where I'd been seen working, based on discussions at the Deaf club.

For example, when I attended hospital appointments to interpret for Deaf patients. -Sat in the waiting area, anybody could misconstrue any informal signed conversations they observed, at any time. So, I learned to remain professional in public places, before assignments began, even if I knew the

90

client well. I could not afford strangers 'eavesdropping' and casting aspersions about my professionalism.

Yet also Invisible

Over time, I became more experienced and familiar with police assignments and protocols. When I'd receive police calls requesting my attendance to interpret, I spoke their language. I answered with my "posh telephone voice," asked pertinent questions, for example, had the detained person requested legal representation (I'd spent too many hours waiting for briefs to arrive, so now I scheduled my arrival with their estimated time of arrival)? If I knew the Custody Sergeant, I would abbreviate their job title to "Sarge." I was even handed the custody suite keys once by a sergeant and sent to make myself a drink in the kitchen. That's how trusted I'd become.

I would always report to the enquiry desk upon arrival at the police station and wait for the Interviewing Officer to meet me and take me down to "custody." However, sometimes, I'd be invisible to the officer despite being in plain view. The officer would repeatedly call out my name, trying to spot an interpreter among the people waiting for their friend or relative to be released. I would look directly at the officer, or with raised eyebrows attempting to convey, "That's me," but they didn't see me. Could it be that their mental construct of what an interpreter looked like, influenced, in part, by how I sounded to them on the telephone, was incongruent with the Black female trying to engage their attention?

Being freelance, naturally, I would advertise my services as an interpreter. The idea of adding photos to directory entries had not yet been conceived. Occasionally, I would receive calls from well-meaning organisers wanting to reflect diversity.

The conversations were almost always formulaic:
My name had been passed on to them because they were holding an event. Insert some generic phrases about equality

and diversity and reflecting the subject, audience or a commitment to 'the cause' and are you available?

I sometimes found it slightly unnerving - especially if the call came on a weekend when I wasn't in work mode. Before even identifying themselves, strangers outside of my network knew my ethnicity and sought to book me, not on my ability, but on the basis that visually, I 'looked the part.'

Depending on who the co-interpreters were, I would accept or decline the booking request. Those I declined included:

An Equality & Diversity Conference
A national organisation running a conference on Equality and Diversity approached me to work with two unqualified, (White) interpreters - one male, one female. They wanted a Black interpreter to complete their diverse representation (that's my inference, not their stated intentions). The interpreters' ethnicity was not the issue; their inexperience and trainee status were. I was a qualified and experienced interpreter but interpreting conferences can be stressful for a number of reasons, including knowledge of the subjects, the presenter's delivery, and pace.

Oh, how I'd try not to roll my eyes when I heard "I'm going to give you a whistle-stop tour..." or that they had a full programme and would try to make up time and shorten lunch. Simultaneous interpreting is mentally tiring, especially given the average concentration span is twenty minutes, before your mind wanders to deadlines, your in-tray and what's in the fridge for dinner tonight.

Mutual support is needed in a conference interpreting team, from people who are equally experienced and possess the knowledge and skills to intuit when and how your co-interpreter needs support.

It was an unequal partnership, ironic given their conference was about equality. As the 'senior' interpreter, the trainee interpreters might implicitly assume that I would take on the lion's share of any challenging parts of the conference. In my opinion, it would be unfair to all parties involved, so I declined.

The Research Talk

Towards the end of my career, I tired of being sought out because event organisers thought it was a good idea to visually represent diversity. An academic reached out looking for a Black interpreter to co-work with their university's in-house interpreter. They were hosting an event to present their research findings. Instead of creating opportunities to truly embed equality and diversity within the research study by recruiting suitably qualified team members, they wanted a stranger for a day.

They had used interpreters throughout their in-depth study. Those interpreters were available to interpret the event, but those interpreters were White. It seemed disingenuous, paying lip service to diversity front of house while failing to address it behind the scenes. It seemed unfair on the co-interpreter, me and the participants to accept the assignment.

Imagine you're back at school and there's a practical science exam. You have the option of being paired with someone who has crammed in their science revision the night before the test, or someone studious who'd been working on their science all year. Who would you rather work with?

The university had interpreters with the skills, experience, and specific subject knowledge, available. This meant speakers could leave information implicit (and research data remain slightly ambiguous) and the interpreters could 'unpack' the intended meaning for the audience, without having to interrupt the speakers to clarify their utterances. It didn't make sense to potentially disrupt the flow of proceedings and dynamics by substituting one of those interpreters with a Black interpreter because it was appropriate to their study.

I spoke out, which wasn't well received by the member organisation who'd sent the request on behalf of the university. I am the type of person who prefers to expose the real issue instead of applying sticking plasters over wounds. The member organisation viewed it as an opportunity and that Black interpreters should be grateful. I saw it as yet another scrap being tossed by people who believed they were helping 'the cause.' I could secure interpreting jobs based on my ability as a competent interpreter, irrespective of my ethnicity.

I didn't need their crumbs, nor did I wish to be complicit in perpetuating the problem.

Oh, you're good [...]
Then there were the organisers who let slip their unconscious bias. They would be surprised that despite seeking out a Black interpreter for their project, I was actually good at my job. Of course, they didn't actually say, "Oh you're good for a Black interpreter," but the ellipses spoke volumes. The surprise was conveyed in their voice, as they managed to catch their prejudiced thought before it escaped their lips, stopping at, "Oh, you're good...!"

I would [politely] make it clear with my facial expression that given my job was to interpret the intent behind language - what people said and what was actually meant - we both understood what had just happened. It seemed that subconsciously some organisers lowered their expectations when they "needed" a Black interpreter for a specific assignment or project.

This happened with some interpreting I did for a project aimed at non-Black parents of deaf children. The film company, acting on behalf of their client, wanted a Black

94

interpreter. After the director declared, "Oh, you're good... I'll consider you for generic projects," I smiled and thanked her, but I had no intention of working with them again. Before we met, she was extremely particular about what I looked like, what my hair looked like, etc. which had nothing to do with continuity, nor my interpreting ability.

"There's one there!"
The worst incident by far had to be interpreting induction training at an NHS Trust. Of course, there were lots of uneventful assignments, most were 'successful' interpretations, some were comical, others tragic and a few truly compromised my safety. However, being Black was not a factor in any of those assignments.

By this point in my career, I had effectively retired from interpreting practice but was still managing the interpreting agency I'd set up. One of our clients had appointed a new staff member to their team, and we were co-ordinating his interpreting support, beginning with the Trust's induction training. The night before, one of the co-interpreters withdrew due to illness. I sent an urgent request to interpreters hoping they had some availability to cover gaps. It also meant me stepping back into the interpreting arena as a practitioner.
I was to cover the morning slot of an equality and diversity day until the interpreter we'd secured could get to the venue once her other assignment ended.

I arrived to find the co-interpreter, and new employee sat near the window, on the other side of the room to the entrance. I started interpreting as the trainer introduced the session. She spoke about how the demographics of the geographical area had changed since the 1980s by making a 'then and now' comparison to the various languages the Trust's information was now translated into.

The trainer explained that the Trust liked to recruit staff who reflected the community which they served, but looking around the room, there were only two or three men present. Then the trainer stated, "We're all White," which I signed. "We're all pale and pasty," at which point, I shot a glance across at my co-interpreter, as I signed it. ."There's nobody here with olive skin." I signed this, then looked at the Deaf client to see if he wanted to sign anything.

Delivering Deaf Awareness Training to colleagues was part of his former job and new job. Perhaps if he'd introduced himself, stating that he'd brought interpreters to facilitate access to information he'd indirectly draw the trainer's attention to the fact that her statements about the people present were factually incorrect.

After another comment about nobody having tanned skin, the trainer declared, "THERE'S ONE THERE!" pointing across at me. Her language use immediately conjured up a racist image in my mind of 'negroes' caught lazing under a banyan tree during colonial times.

I was horrified. But worse was yet to come. This fifty- or sixty-year-old Equality and Diversity trainer employed by an NHS Trust then walked across to me, came up behind my chair and grabbed my arms. I wasn't able to sign while she was hugging me. Then she started talking to me! Interpreters cannot engage in a conversation while interpreting dialogue between other parties. You're already juggling information between two languages - one spoken and one signed - simultaneously using your short-term memory and operating a time lag (always helpful when searching for cultural and linguistic equivalents in the target language so what's intended in the source language makes sense).

Moreover, just when I thought it couldn't get any worse, this woman whom I'd never met, nor spoken to before, planted a kiss in the middle of my forehead! This was a first. In all of my seventeen years of interpreting, this had never happened before. I had no schema to deal with this situation and so, I... laughed. Nervously. No words, just laughter. Throughout this interaction, the room had remained awkwardly silent. All the participants were facing the front, so they were able to see the signing taking place. The trainer was facing her audience, and we were off to the side, so she was oblivious to my presence. It was evident from her telling me that she hadn't seen me and I must have "snuck in" under her nose.

The Deaf client didn't help matters by adding, "Interpreters are invisible anyway," which is associated with an outdated model of interpreting. When the interpreting profession began, a conduit model was taught, it encouraged perceptions of interpreters as non-participants. Times and models have changed to reflect that communication facilitated by interpreters is filtered through their experience and map of the world. Therefore, interpreters in constructing meaning between parties who don't share the same language, are equal participants in co-creating the dialogue.

What went through my head was:

-   This is an induction training - first impressions last.
-   The Deaf person will continue to experience a lack of access to information, as access is often an afterthought when people lack awareness.
-   As a cultural and linguistic mediator between a marginalised and historically oppressed group and members representative of a majority (non-deaf) society, would my views reflect on the minority status client?
-   An interpreter can help people who cannot sign to feel more comfortable around Deaf people and ease interactions or use language and attitude to exclude

others who don't understand sign language and Deaf culture.
- All the participants are new employees; I don't want this situation to become awkward for them, too.
- I won't have the opportunity to address this, as I'll sneak out once the other interpreter arrives.
- I'm already out of the interpreting game. The likelihood of encountering this woman again are remote.
- It wasn't the time nor the place to have a conversation with the Deaf client about newer models of interpreting approaches.

My co-interpreter said to me that I handled it better than her friends, who are Black, would.
After I left, I was angry with myself that I hadn't dealt with it more satisfactorily.

I followed up with the Trust's referrer who'd requested the support on behalf of their new employee. They replied that the E&D trainer always "put her foot in it." Had I been an employee of the Trust, I would've expressed at the time that her behaviour was inappropriate. I would have asserted that an Equality & Diversity session was the right place to have a discussion about conduct and language. But I wasn't an employee.

How would other Black women deal with the situation? To be honest, I don't know. I can only share my own experiences. I grew up in a Northern former textile town where there weren't many Black people. I preferred male company and then when I began my professional career, my counterparts were largely Caucasian women. By telling our stories, we can understand where experiences and coping strategies are shared experiences among Black women. Collectively, we can bring about change.

Why Black Girl Magic is a Thing

Roianne Nedd

A comment that someone made on my LinkedIn profile inspired this blog. I had shared a story about the pay gap for Black women, and someone commented Bullsh%*. In a way, I wasn't surprised, the experiences of Black women are often hidden in gender stories that focus more on White women or lost in case studies about racism which disproportionately focus on Black men's experiences.

Reflecting on the casual abuse, I had received I was going to call this blog "Why I hate being a Black woman" but frankly I don't. Being a Black woman puts me into an identity space that is as complex as it is unique and frankly it's a magical place to be. Furthermore, when I mentioned this blog to a friend of mine using the title "Why I hate being a Black woman" she said "Really? But who or what else would you be?" And she's right who would I be? The answer quite simply is no one. This is my destiny and my birthright, and as part of my journey, I have chosen to help other people understand why Black women deserve to be valued as much as anyone else and to give an insight into the experience of being a Black woman.

Well let's start with a definition magic according to the Google dictionary magic means "the power of influencing events by using mysterious or supernatural forces." I'm not suggesting that all Black women have supernatural powers or that they are witches but what am I unequivocally saying is that Black women are forced to influence almost everyone they encounter. Black women are forced to be chameleons and mind readers to gain success, and it's this unique combination of race and gender that sparked Kimberle Crenshaw's work on intersectionality.

Maybe I sound a little dramatic but let me tell you about the four distinct groups who have an impact on Black women as leaders and business women and how we could all be more aware of how these relationships can be both negative and positive.

White men- let's start with the powerhouse. White men hold most of the influence in business and industry, and as a result, they have the chance to have a major impact. As a Black woman, I've been lucky to have the mentorship sponsorship of some very senior white male leaders, but equally early in my career, I also had the misfortune of working with a white male leader whose misogyny was only exceeded by his racism.

He actively belittled my efforts, didn't invest in my development and openly favoured the white women in the team. It became clear within a brief time that for my career to flourish I would need to leave that team and so I requested a transfer. The reason for my transfer was an open secret, and I was asked to see the group director once my transfer was agreed ostensibly to say goodbye.

I remember walking with him as we talked. He was another influential white man. He asked me whether the rumours about why I was leaving were true. I was happy to know that he had heard, and I confirmed to him the experiences that myself and other ethnic minority women had faced at the hands of this man. This director, a quiet yet imposing man, walked beside me in silence, a thoughtful look on his face as he listened. When I was finished venting, I fell silent, and we continued walking.

As we neared our destination, he turned to me, took my hand shook it and thanked me for leaving without a fuss. That conversation had a lasting impact on me. As a Black woman, I'm expected to acquiesce and to "not make a fuss" if I want to progress. Standing up for myself and others are interpreted by some as histrionics and drama, and no one wants to deal with that. The lesson I learnt though was that I needed to refine my intuitive skills so that I would recognize quickly the people who would perceive me as too much like hard work.

White women - In most organisations, this group are the second most influential. Much like their male counterparts, they have the chance to be great fulcrums for change or to make things more difficult for Black women. Think of colonialism and slavery. The impact of White women in those days is a relatively little recognised and highlighted issue. White women are put on a societal pedestal, and sadly some of them use that privilege to elevate themselves on the backs of women who don't look like them. I call it the damsel in distress phenomena which plays out in workplaces all the time. I'll give you two examples:

1. I've been walking with a White male colleague who would hold doors open for White women but not afford me the same courtesy because my blackness negates my femininity. I'm sure other Black women have experienced something similar.
2. As a Black woman, I know I must do better. I know I must work harder but like anyone else I have limits and sometimes I have conceded that my workload is too heavy. I remember doing this a few years ago, explaining why I couldn't take on more work and being given a "pep" talk by my White female manager as she patiently explained that she had every confidence that I could do it. She had fundamentally misunderstood my issue was capacity, not capability. A few days later a White female colleague bemoaned her "heavy" workload in the team meeting. Our manager rallied the troops immediately "recognising" that my colleague needed help.

These two examples show how difficult it can be working with some White women whether as colleagues or managers. Their needs will always be superior to yours and your calls for

103

parity will be ignored or mistaken for jealousy and envy. Sadly, policy has reinforced this with the Davies Review failing to address that women aren't a homogenous group and therefore diversity and intersectionality should have been fundamental principles enshrined in the targets for female progression.

Black men - It saddens me even to type the words that some Black men can be problematic for Black women, but in some cases, they are. This challenge is due to traditional views of gender which means that some Black men find strong, ambitious and independent Black women challenging. They feel threatened, and they feel that fundamentally a woman's place is supplementary to a man's. In the workplace, this can have impacts on structures such as Employee Resource Groups if the leader is a Black male who isn't advocating for the progression of all Black people. I know one of these men, he created a structure where women did the work while he took the spotlight and the credit. Because of his charisma and magnetism, it was easy to get swept away by him, but after a while, the veneer faded, and his sexism was clear.

Other Black women - This is one of the most complex groups to navigate and belong to. Internally as a group we represent so many identities. My identity is also contextual depending on who I'm talking to and where I am. In Guyana, I'm a "Dougla" (someone mixed with East Indian and Black), in the UK I'm Black, and to some Jamaican people, I'm "coolie." While I'm comfortable with being these things, I'm most comfortable being me. I sometimes struggle to "fit in" within groups of Black women. In the past, I've felt and been told: "I'm not Black enough." I'm not conforming to the norms of the stereotypical Black female leader.

My cultural context means that I'm also close to my East Indian roots leading to confusion and assumptions about my authenticity as a Black woman in the UK. I also watch as people expect certain things from me and when I don't present as angry, loud, aggressive or grateful I can feel the confusion and consternation emanating from them. Because I do not neatly fit into the stereotypical Black woman box and frankly I never will because my strongest identity is Roianne Nedd. I love being one of a kind. Conformity is not one of my aspirations and like we say in Guyana "I was born alone" so I don't need anyone's approval to be me. Professionally, integrity overrides friendship.

So back to my original point Black women are powerful and magical. We navigate relationships having to hone our intuition so that we can recognise the people who will have positive impacts on us but also aware that there are people in the above four groups who can be active or passive detractors. Any successful Black woman has assessed her territory and will be able to articulate their experiences of navigating relationships.

So next time you meet a Black woman lean away from your biases, ask her name and get to know her. Look beyond her race and her gender and understand the magical being in front of you.

To close, I'm going to share a quote from Jessie Williams that I fell in love with the moment I heard it.

"Just because we're magic doesn't mean we're not real."

****First published on LinkedIn in September 2017

How to Build Your Own Brand
Collette Philip, Managing Director, Brand by Me.

In this book, we've read about the stereotypes that are assigned to Black women in the workplace. The tired clichés that prevent Black women from getting ahead, showing their strengths and being themselves at work. This is an issue for the individual and employer alike. The individual is robbed of opportunities to demonstrate the unique assets they bring to their role. The employer loses out on the potential of that employee. Instead of a happy, productive and fulfilled team member, they have a disillusioned, dispirited and disenfranchised worker who is only focused on getting through the day unscathed and unburdened by the weight of these assumptions.

As a Black woman in advertising (a predominantly White and male industry), I laboured under the weight of these stereotypes for years. For example, I was told I was 'too assertive' when I expressed my opinion to senior management, yet 'too accommodating' if I tried to make sure the needs of my clients were met.

The clichés of being Black and being a woman were used as reasons not to promote me or give me the opportunities that others readily received merely because my face didn't fit. How do I know this? Because I run my own brand consultancy and the strengths I demonstrated then are the reasons our clients love working with us now.

So, what do we do about this?
- How do we move past the clichés so that Black women can be their brilliant best at work?
- How do we enable our strengths to shine so that we can do things in our own, distinctive way?
- How do we make sure that our work is aligned with our values so that we feel a sense of purpose at work?

One way of overcoming these challenges is to build a strong personal brand. The concept of personal branding has become something of a buzzword, attached to the notion of having a public persona that draws thousands of followers on social media. But that's not actually what a personal brand is.

Your personal brand is how you define and articulate who you are, what you stand for and how you deliver this in your own way. It's how you bring together your purpose in life and your values, along with your personality and strengths. It allows you to pursue and achieve your ambitions in a way that's authentic to you. It is something you can develop and present to others so that they have an expectation of who you are and how you do it differently from the rest.

Sounds good, right? Imagine being so clear on who you are at work, that people not only 'just get you,' but you are given opportunities because of it. So clear that you are hired specifically, not just because you can meet the skills required and deliver the tasks, but because your personality and values are seen as an asset to the team and company.

This is the power of building a personal brand in the workplace. And it's not just great for Black women, It is useful for all employees and therefore for employers too. Encouraging your employees to understand their personal brands means they will be more self-aware, able to play to their strengths and also respect and enhance the strengths of others. It means that people will feel free to be open, versus hiding behind limiting assumptions and beliefs.

So how do you develop your personal brand?
It starts by understanding what you're great at and how you're different. Make a list of your strengths and pick out the things that you're both great at and love to do. From there, think about how you do these things differently to other people. What makes you stand out? Once you have defined these

characteristics, consider how they benefit the world around you. Why does the world need what you do best?

The other aspect of your personal brand to consider is your values. Companies often articulate their values. So, it's imperative that we know our personal values, so we can make sure there's no conflict. We may value many things. But in this context, our values are the non-negotiable principles that drive how we work. The principles that we hold so dear that we never want to give them up, no matter how much we're paid or who is asking us to. Understanding your personal brand means being clear on your values.

This, of course, is just a starting point. But it will help you start to define your personal brand.

Most importantly remember that we all have a personal brand. For many Black women, it's a collection of clichés, assumptions, and stereotypes that are assigned to us. It's time to define our own personal brands in the workplace. And it's the responsibility of good employers to help us do it.

Trusted Black Girl CPD for Inclusive Leaders

So, you've read the book, and you're wondering what to do next. Here are eight things that you can do to continue and broaden your journey as an inclusive leader

1. Find out if you have any unconscious biases in relation to ethnicity
2. Discuss your potential biases with an objective third party such as a coach or mentor
3. Reflect on your leadership style by carrying out a personal assessment. I recommend the SHINE model (page 115)
4. Educate yourself through books, podcasts, and events that focus on different perspectives
5. Become a vocal ally to minority groups, not just a passive bystander.
6. Learn how to support and encourage other leaders to be inclusive
7. Challenge inappropriate behaviour
8. Change the way you host meetings so that everyone's voice can be heard

Giving Thanks

Special thanks to the following people for their support and contributions

- ❖ Andrea Rowe
- ❖ C Don
- ❖ Collette Philip
- ❖ Jacqueline. A.Hinds
- ❖ Jonathan Ashong-Lamptey
- ❖ Kate Franklin
- ❖ Kate Isichei
- ❖ Lara Yusuf
- ❖ Mairi McHaffie
- ❖ MaryFay Tita-Kuna
- ❖ Mbeke Waseme
- ❖ Michelle Delices
- ❖ N Williams
- ❖ Rob Berkeley
- ❖ Ruth Pearson
- ❖ Tricia Mitchell
- ❖ Tanya Galliara

SHINE – The Inclusive Leadership Self-Assessment Tool

Developed by consultants working together at RoCaro the **SHINE Inclusive Leadership Self-Assessment** helps you to create a vision for the type of inclusive leader that you want to be, There is no right answer. This tool only requires that you answer each question being honest with yourself and reflecting on your answers and deciding your next steps.

Strengths – what are your strengths? What makes you a good leader? Are you an inclusive leader?

Hopes – What are your inclusive leadership aspirations? What type of leader do you want to be? What does inclusive leadership mean to you?

Improve – what do you need to improve to become an even more inclusive leader?

Nurture – how will you make the changes necessary to improve your style?

Embed – how will you know that your inclusive leadership style is improving?

If you would like to book a confidential coaching session to go through your SHINE results or to help you to do the SHINE Assessment, please contact team@RoCaro.co.uk

About the Author

Roianne Nedd is a Diversity and Inclusion expert, life coach and author. She is passionate and dedicated to helping organisations to embrace the principles of diversity and inclusion and focuses on intersectional feminism, unconscious bias, and inclusive leadership.

She has built an impressive range of skills and experience since starting her career in a busy County Court in Central London, working in various roles within Central Government including Change Management, Communications and Diversity, and Inclusion. While working, she qualified as a Chartered Accountant and gained her Post Graduate Certificate in Leadership using these skills to round her approach to driving inclusion in businesses.

In the latter part of her career, she worked as an objective advisor and consultant to companies in a range of industries including financial and professional services, retail banking, central and local government, engineering and tech to provide innovative solutions and training packages on D&I to clients.

Most recently she has focused on building a range of inclusion interventions including benchmarking tools and unconscious bias seminars delivered through her consultancy business RoCaro.

In her spare time, Roianne runs Women of Kaieteur, a global empowerment network supporting Guyanese women. She is also a self-appointed Amplifier of Women's voices helping them find their purpose, unleash their passion and maximise their potential through her life-coaching work and authorship of nine books including self-help book The Cracked Cocoon Principles.

About the Publisher

Welcome to True Voice Publishing (formally RHJ Publishing and a trading name of ROI Jelly Ltd). Following some years in the publishing business, the rebranded True Voice publishing launched in January 2017.

Embodying the values of our founder, True Voice Publishing exists to help writers share their stories and find and amplify their authentic voices.

At True Voice, we want to share **HIS**tory and **HER**story.

The stories that we share come in all shapes and sizes and we celebrate the eclectic mix of voices and mediums that we use.

We work both formally and informally with writers and creatives to tell their stories and find the best way to share their craft.

We also take immense pleasure in working with the next generation of writers by mentoring, supporting and empowering EVERYONE to find their voice.

About RoCaro

Introducing RoCaro a social enterprise built to provide flexible Diversity and Inclusion resourcing to meet your needs.

We are a social enterprise with three main ethical objectives:

- To make UK workplaces fairer and more welcoming for minority groups, e.g., women, ethnic minorities, LGBT+
- To champion and advocate for gender equality for women and men in the workplace and beyond by amplifying our voice in these issues and supporting charitable efforts to effect social change
- To capacity build our client organisations so that they develop knowledge about diversity and inclusion to the extent that it becomes business as usual for them

Crucially we are not a membership organisation. We operate through subscriptions and credits and traditional consultancy days. Clients pay for the support that they need. We actively encourage you to use our skills, maximise your benefit and receive value for money.

To this end we offer

- Flexible packages incorporating a menu of services for you to choose from
- quarterly, half yearly and annual subscriptions
- The ability to roll over unused credits
- Virtual support to underpin face to face interaction
- Bespoke packages on demand
- Packages to suit varied sizes and types of organisation

- Template tools, policies, and documents to save you time and money
- Regular insights into industry trends and best practice
-

Why not get in touch to find out how we can help you to embed equality diversity and inclusion into your organisation without busting your budget.

Email: Team@RoCaro.co.uk

Website: www.RoCaro.co.uk
Twitter   @RoCaroConsults
Facebook   www.facebook.com/RoCaroConsulting